Enjoying Pictures

London
Routledge & Kegan Paul

Enjoying
Pictures

First published in 1975
by Routledge & Kegan Paul Ltd
Broadway House, 68–74 Carter Lane,
London EC4V 5EL
Filmset and printed in Great Britain by
BAS Printers Limited, Wallop, Hampshire
ISBN 0 7100 8088 3

Frontispiece : View at Auvers. *Vincent van Gogh (1853–90)*

Contents

'. . . all the business of life is to endeavour to find out what you don't know by what you do'

John Whiting *Marching Song*

Editor's preface

Most of us are surrounded by so many pictures that very often we do not even look at them. Our eyes can only take in a certain amount and whether we *see* a picture depends upon whether we are willing to try to find out what the person who made it is saying.

This book is written to help you to explore and to discover a lot about pictures that you may never have noticed before. It does not tell you which pictures are 'good' and which are not, for no two people see and enjoy exactly the same thing. Our eyes differ as much as our interests, our needs and our experience, but unless we know a little about what to look for, we miss a great deal.

If you are planning to do a project about pictures you will have to use your eyes and your imagination. You will need to talk to people who make pictures and to those who buy them, either for themselves or for others. You may decide to make a study of one favourite picture, or the work of one particular artist; the work done in a certain country or district may interest you especially, or you may wish to look into some technical aspect of what pictures are for and how people make them. In any case this book will be useful and will help you decide how to start exploring and how to divide up your work. Don't forget to make your work look as clear and pleasant as you can; think over whether a loose-leaf arrangement might be best, because then you can add extra sections when you like, without altering the parts that are finished.

The most important idea in this book is in the title — ENJOYING pictures. Once you begin to look carefully at pictures of all sorts you may find that they become a life-long interest and enjoyment.

M.H.

Thinking about pictures 1

The world is full of pictures. When you go into the street you can see large posters on hoardings or smaller ones in shop windows. At home there may be pictures hanging on the walls. Newspapers and magazines, calendars and comics are full of pictures. There are illustrations in books and on picture postcards; pictures in railway stations or airports, in tubes and buses. You will find them in schools, in shops, in churches, in museums and art galleries, in public buildings sometimes, and on stamps.

There they are, all over the place, and do you, I wonder, ever look at them? There are so many different kinds and all tell different stories. Even those that seem to be nothing but a coloured pattern tell a story though perhaps it may be a little difficult at first to understand what it is all about.

What is a picture?
Painting, like writing or talking, dancing or making music, is a way of saying something — of expressing yourself. If you want to tell a story really well, you must arrange your thoughts to make a plot — maybe it is true or maybe you imagine it, it does not matter — then you carefully choose words to convey your meaning and you make the whole into a sort of pattern, so that the story becomes fascinating and interesting.

With a picture you do the same sort of thing. Only instead of words and paragraphs and chapters and punctuation, you use colours and lines and shapes and textures which you can make into a pattern.

1 Feeding the
Elephant. *Anon.
(Moghul c. 1620)
In the early sixteenth
century the Moghuls
invaded India and
founded an empire.
Akba, one of its
greatest emperors,
loved painting and
encouraged artists to
paint scenes from
everyday life, not only
religious subjects as
before. Elephants were
held in high respect
and even loved, for
they could be trained.
What can you tell
from the picture about
this one?*

When people want to paint pictures, they have to learn their craft, as a cabinet-maker has to learn his if he wants to make a chair or a cupboard, or if an instrument-maker wants to make a piano or a guitar. Just sometimes, people, particularly children, are so excited about what they want to paint that they can make a picture without much craftsmanship and yet it can be very lively and even beautiful.

To make a good copy of something you see in front of you — a vase of flowers or a person or whatever — is not necessarily making a good picture. An artist may copy a lot of things as an exercise, so that he gets their shape and structure and colour into his mind's eye. It is rather like learning to play scales if one wants to play the piano. However well the scales are played, they themselves do not make a piece of music.

All art is a kind of magic, where you turn certain things, like colours and shapes and lines into something quite different. A painting can do much more than a photograph can do, even a coloured one. Photography can be both important and useful, sometimes even beautiful, but it is of a different order.

A painting can make you *feel* as well as *see* something: it can

2 Portrait of a Man. *Titian (1487/90–1576) This portrait is far more than a copy of the sitter. The artist is telling you what he felt about his character too.*

stir the imagination, it can make you feel pleased, excited or quiet, happy or sad, it can carry you into worlds which you had no idea existed. It can surprise you or make you laugh and it can puzzle or mystify you. Paintings can make fun of people or events, can carry you right into a dream or fantasy or be so factual that you can recognise something of your own everyday life in them.

If ten artists were given the same subject to paint, each one would do it differently from the others. This is because they would not be painting the subject only, but, because each one of us is different and individual, they would also be painting their own thoughts and feelings and ideas about the subject. The camera is a mechanical instrument that records what is in front of it. We are human beings and we put into our pictures what we *feel* as well as what we see. This is the beginning of what we call style. I shall talk about this a little later on.

You will enjoy looking at pictures more, if you try and paint some yourself. Even if you think you are not very successful, it does not matter, for it will give you an idea of both the pleasures and the difficulties that other artists have had.

Looking and seeing

Often we see something but do not look at it. Now that sounds like nonsense but it is quite true. For instance, we are waiting to cross a road; we see a car coming and stop. But often we do not look at it. When it has passed, do we know what the car looked like? Was it a saloon or an estate, was it new and shining, or old and shabby, what was the make, the colour or the number? If we are thinking of just getting across the road safely, we probably will not bother. We have *seen* the car, but have not *looked* at it.

We may come into a room and see a picture on the wall, but do we notice it any more than we notice a chair standing in a corner? Usually we do not. The chair, at least, may suddenly become useful, if more people come into the room, and it is pulled out for someone to sit on. The picture only becomes useful if you look at it and absorb it. So seeing and looking at something are two quite different things. As our eyes are open most of the day, we see thousands of things: we become so familiar with most of them that we rarely look at them.

Do you look at your mother, for instance? She is not quite the same every day. She changes; sometimes she may look gay and sprightly, her hair prettily done and her eyes bright and sparkling. At other times she may look tired or worried or impatient, or full of inward thoughts, so her face will not look the same, even her hair or her movements may be different. Do you notice this?

To look at things with your mind (so to speak), as well as with your eyes, is quite different from just seeing something.

3 Still Life. *Fernand Leger (1881–1955) (© by S.P.A.D.E.M., Paris, 1974)* This is an unusual view of objects in a still life. The artist, instead of painting them as the eye would see them, has made them into a pattern where colour masses, straight and wavy lines, dots and stripes all play their part. There is no 'ought' in painting: the imagination is just as important as fact. The mind is not a camera: it can play around with lines and shapes and colours as it pleases. The important thing in the end, is that it produces a fascinating picture.

It is like hearing and listening. You can hear someone playing the piano or the guitar, but are you listening to the music? On the whole it is easier to *listen* to music than to *look* at a picture. Because music more easily touches our feelings and we can listen to a tune and enjoy it without a great deal of effort. But to get the full pleasure of it we have to try to understand, to get to know something about the music. This does need effort. It means listening a lot and listening carefully. Both the composer and the painter are trying to say something to us. Sometimes it is worth saying, sometimes it isn't, sometimes we just don't understand it. It is a two-way traffic; the artist gets his ideas from the happenings in life around him. For instance, he may see horses jump at a Horse Show and find that not only are the horses themselves thrilling but also the curious and wonderful lines the actual jumps describe in the air are equally exciting. These lines and the horses' movement work upon him so strongly that he feels he must invent a picture of what he has seen. If you look at the picture he has made, and if you want to enjoy and understand it, you will need to make some effort yourself — go out towards it — putting yourself to some extent into the artist's mind and mood and trying to allow the painting itself to talk to you.

*4 A Concert.
Lorenzo Costa
(c. 1460–1535)
Here you see three
quite ordinary people
making music together
and enjoying it.
Notice how the
placing of the hands
repeats the line of
heads and shoulders,
while the outside arms
seem to hold the
picture together.*

Different kinds of pictures

Just as there are all kinds of music — dance music or songs, marching music or music to celebrate a great occasion, music that is gay or calm or can give us a sense of wonder or of excitement — so there are different kinds of pictures.

Some can give us a sense of satisfaction, like a well-designed sign, stamp or poster; some can tell us an enthralling story, or a joke; others can express protest or unrest, or excitement or joy — in fact there is nothing that painting cannot express, so long as the artist has the feeling, the talent and the skill to do it.

It is therefore very well worth while taking the trouble to try and find out what pictures give you real pleasure. And as we ourselves are many-sided creatures, we shall probably find we like different sorts of pictures. They can do a lot for us. They can widen our experience and deepen our feelings, make us more observant and understanding. Often the artist can state something clearly, that we ourselves have felt only vaguely, but could not express. He can give us a lot of joy. Isn't this something worth while? It can affect our whole life.

2   Why people paint pictures

Pictures through the ages

Signs, symbols and advertisements

Making up your mind about pictures

Not only in England but all over the world pictures have been painted. At all times, and for all sorts of different reasons.

Pictures through the ages

Prehistoric people painted in their caves or on rocks. Eskimos in their igloos scratched fascinating patterns and pictures on their tools made of walrus tusks or bones. Red Indians of Central America made pictures of their gods on the ground with coloured sands; Egyptians painted the walls of their tombs; the Chinese painted on silk or fine paper; the Greeks painted stories of their gods and heroes on their beautiful pots; the inside of a Roman house at the time of Caesar would, more often than not, be adorned with pictures painted on the walls. Scythians, who were nomads, ornamented their gorgeous golden bridles and other horse trappings with wonderful engraved designs. The Scandinavians wove stories and legends into their blankets and rugs. Aborigines in Australia painted pictures on tree bark, on burial poles and even on each others' bodies.

Arabs and Indians, Persians and Turks all painted pictures and illustrated books. All Europeans from very early times have always painted pictures. There was a time when every church in England, big or small, was covered with paintings. Pictures of exciting stories from the Bible, and often too, pictures of everyday life, a kind of strip cartoon of ploughing, sowing, reaping, hunting, shooting, fishing and playing games.

5 and 6 Symbol of London Transport. Symbol for British Rail. These are such simple designs and so apt, that it is impossible to forget them. We call signs like this symbols, because they mean something. London Transport is saying: we take you round London, but we also take you a little way out of it. The British Rail symbol indicates that trains go, and come, and are swift. The arrow-like shapes put that into our minds.

In fact pictures were made for use and pleasure long before writing was invented and before reading was common.

And of course today, people still are painting pictures, but about quite different sorts of things. That's natural, isn't it, because we live different sorts of lives.

Signs and symbols

If you go along a main road now, you will see signs that are pictures of a sort. It is easier and simpler to explain things by making a picture than by using words. If you want a motorist to be warned that he is coming to a small bridge, a sign is put up showing a drawing of a hump-backed bridge; or if there is danger of cattle or sheep straying across unfenced roads, a drawing of a cow or sheep is displayed. How much easier for the eye to take this in quickly than if one had to read a lot of words.

Cattle   **Hump bridge**

7 Here are two of the very many road signs we see everywhere now. How simple they are, but how effectively they remind us to drive carefully.

In towns all sorts of pictures are used for telling you something. I wonder if you can find other signs and symbols, either giving a

8 London's Fairs.
*William Roberts
(1895–   ) The
hustle, noise and fun
of a fair is very well
shown in these posters.
Notice how the type is
well designed to go
with the poster itself.*

warning or an order, in the streets or lanes round your home. Perhaps you can find some on motorways, canals or rivers.

Advertisements

Posters and advertisements can be fascinating too (though some are very silly). All of them have something to say. They tell us of things for sale, from cars to soft drinks. They tell us of places we can visit; of films or plays to be seen; or pills to take for certain ills.

Look at them and try and make up your mind whether they tell their story well or badly, and whether the pictures make you stop and look at them. Perhaps you would like to begin making a collection of posters and pictures from all over the world.

LONDON HISTORY AT THE

LONDON MUSEUM

DOVER STREET
OR ST. JAMES'S PARK STATION

9 London History.
(E. McKnight Kauffer
(1890–1954)
All the excitement of
the Great Fire of
London is shown in
this simple poster.
Notice how the whole
design is helped by
the carefully placed
lettering at the base.

Why we paint pictures

As I have said, pictures are painted for a whole lot of different reasons. Sometimes to tell a simple story, sometimes because the artist had very strong feelings about something – for instance, faith in God, or winning battles and killing your enemy – sometimes because he loved something very much or had strange dreams and fantasies.

It all starts with using your eye and your mind's eye, which is the imagination. The sight of ships in a harbour at sunset, or a mother holding her baby, or apples on a plate, or a hot sunny day in the fields or a great terrifying storm over mountains, and a thousand others things can make people want to paint them.

10 Stamps can remind us visually of anniversaries and special events, and are attractive for our letters — and our collections. Anniversary stamps designed by Fritz Wegner to commemorate the discovery of Tutankhamun's tomb in 1922 and to mark the 100th anniversary of the Rugby Football Union. Christmas stamp for 1972 designed by Sally Stiff

Let us forget, for the time being, the signs and posters and advertisements: these things are indeed very useful and they can be well or badly done; but no one can get really excited over saying, 'Mr Snooks' sausages are the best in the world' or 'Try Poggles' Indigestion Tablets', can they? But you can get both interested and excited about other sorts of pictures.

Making up your mind about pictures

Have you ever been in your local art gallery and looked at some of the paintings there or perhaps visited a special exhibition? Perhaps you have found a painting you liked. Did you think about it or make a note of it or perhaps try to copy it or take a photograph of it? What, I wonder, pleased you? Would you like to have a painting of that sort at home? Not every picture is suitable to have in a room, some only look right in big places, like churches, schools or other public buildings. Some, though, look fine in a room.

Possibly you did not find any you liked, maybe they looked old-fashioned or dull or so odd and strange you could not make them out at all. Try looking at some books of paintings in your public library, especially coloured ones, and see if you can find

some that you enjoy. The Librarian will help you to choose some.
Start by looking at a book on Impressionist pictures. Then try
one on older and then more recent pictures.

If you do not like a picture it does not mean it is a bad picture.
It just means you don't like it. To judge pictures one must have
some experience of looking at them. If you want to judge
anything, whether it is horses or a soccer game or clothes, you
have to have a whole lot of experience before you can tell the
good from the not so good. So, if you dislike or like a picture,
go and look at it often. Gradually you will find out why you like
or dislike it.

Maybe the painting you do not like is about something that

11 Lock and Cottages
on the Stour. *John
Constable (1776–
1837). (Victoria and
Albert Museum. Crown
Copyright.)*
*How lovely this picture
is, looking as fresh
today as when it was
painted. Do you think
it has any special
English qualities
about it?*

may seem strange to you, or is done in a way you don't understand. Perhaps the artist is saying something a bit difficult.

So it is best to start with something you really like. Then you can
say, 'I like that picture', rather than, 'That is a good picture'.
One's likes and dislikes often change with time. When I was
little I hated kippers; I like them very much now. There are some
things, I am sure, that can always satisfy you. But as you grow
older, your tastes change and your understanding widens, and
you can enjoy and absorb more and more.

Telling a story 3

Everybody enjoys a good story. In the past, when there were no books, story-telling was a profession, and people waited eagerly for the story-teller to come round. He would ride or walk from town to town, from village to village, gathering and inventing and then telling stories in the inns or on village greens or in the hall of the local castle or palace. Sometimes he had a lute or guitar slung around his shoulder and told his stories as songs or ballads accompanied by music. Today we watch television or go to the cinema.

Different ways of telling a story
But, as we have pointed out before, there are other ways of story-telling. Instead of using words, stories can be drawn and painted; and these of course would be more permanent. You do not have to remember them, they are always there to be looked at.

History and legend
Sometimes they would be painted, sometimes woven into tapestries or embroidered on cloth. One of the most famous stories in the world was embroidered on yards and yards of linen cloth. It told the whole history of the invasion of England in 1066 by William I — William the Conqueror. It told of the intrigues beforehand, the betrayals and meetings, the ships

12 Part of the Bayeux Tapestry (eleventh century)
British ships draw near the French coast and a sailor prepares to drop anchor.
Note the border of animals, trees and birds.

13 Part of the Bayeux Tapestry
Harold (left centre), his eye pierced by an arrow, is struck down. The last
stand by his army collapses. Notice the mythical creatures in the upper border
and in the lower a soldier stealing a coat of mail from a fallen enemy.

bearing the soldiers crossing the Channel, the great Battle of Hastings itself, King Harold shot in the eye by an arrow, and the eventual crowning of William. You can see how the knights and soldiers and sailors were dressed and armed, what weapons they carried, what kinds of ships they used, what animals they took with them and what the English and Norman soldiers looked like, and even the fish in the sea. It was designed and embroidered in England, not very long after the event, but later was sent to France. It is a magnificent piece of work and was, for hundreds of years, hidden in a great chest. The whole embroidery has now been cleaned and repaired and is on view in Bayeux in Normandy. One day you must go and look at it for yourself. It is like a news-reel of 900 years ago. But with much more fascinating detail than in the average news-reel.

But many other famous stories have been painted and preserved for us to see and enjoy. Different artists very often painted the same story, so you can see different versions and even different ideas of what happened.

The story of St George and the Dragon has been painted many times and the story of Paris stealing the beautiful Helen of Greece and carrying her off to Troy. There is a lovely painting of

14 The Procession of the Wooden Horse into Troy. *Domenico Tiepolo (1727–1804) Do you know about the story this picture depicts? Here Tiepolo has translated the dramatic excitement of the moment into the almost violent activity of the people.*

15 St George and the Dragon. *Paolo Uccello (1396–1475)*
What other paintings of this legend have you seen? How do they differ from this one?

this story in the National Gallery in London, by an Italian painter, a follower of Fra Angelico. It might be interesting to visit there one day and find this picture, and see how the reds and pinks give an air of excitement and movement to the scene. There are scores of other pictures there telling stories, but only look at one or two at a time, or you will get bewildered and confused.

Of course, some artists tell stories in their pictures today too, Stanley Spencer told his own version of Jesus walking through Jerusalem, and Paul Nash painted a wonderful picture of a great mass of fallen and broken aeroplanes, called *The Dead Sea*. They are both in the Tate Gallery in London.

There is no end to the stories that artists have told. Notice how they use their colours to stress a point or to create a mood.

Imagination and fact

To get the fullest understanding of his story, try and find out by looking carefully at what the painter meant, and wanted to say, If you think you have discovered the clue to the picture, do you think he was successful or do you think he could have done better? Do you think you yourself could have done better? Try and see if you can.

When the artist's imagination catches fire, he feels he must find a way of expressing what he feels and what fills his mind. To do this he needs not only all his carefully-learnt craft, but also that spark which is impossible to describe, but which shows itself in so many different ways; no less in an inspired kick in football than in the special manner in which an artist chooses to paint his particular story.

There is no end to the kind of stories that people want to paint. They may be quite simple, perhaps about a little girl who is lost, sad and bewildered. Maybe about some bottles on a table that seem to have something to say to each other. Or they can be quite complicated like some great battle scene or a splendid

16 The Rape of Helen. *A follower of Fra Angelico (c. 1387–1455) How different this painting is from the last one. The artist is showing Paris, the Trojan prince, carrying off the beautiful Helen from her palace in Greece. In the left background is the ship that will carry them to Troy.*

17 Madonna of the Iris. *Ascribed to Albrecht Dürer (1471–1528)*
What an unusual picture of the Madonna and child this is ! She is feeding her
Infant and her expression, so sweet and tender, foreshadows nothing but
tranquillity and happiness for her child. The glimpse we get of the calm sea
and evening sky, through the broken arch, seems to repeat this idea.

deer hunt by night in the forest, all lit up by torches, which you can see at the Ashmolean Museum in Oxford.

18 Night Hunt. *Paolo Uccello (1396–1475) (Ashmolean Museum, Oxford)*

Have you ever read a ghost story that sends shivers down your spine, or a thrilling science fiction story? And did you not enjoy fairy stories, with their witches and ogres and wonderful adventures, when you were little? The world is full of fantasy and make-believe and how much drearier and duller it would be without them.

These stories are not true in the sense that bread and butter on your tea-plate is true. But in another sense they are as much part of us as are our thoughts and feelings. Just as writers have imagined all sorts of strange creatures — devils and spirits, gods and goddesses, angels and fairies, giants and monsters, magicians and sorcerers — some evil and some merely mischievous, about whom they often make up the most magnificent stories, so artists have made remarkable pictures out of their imagination. This boundless world of fantasy enriches our lives and stimulates our own imagination.

Also painters have invented pictures of events that happened hundreds or even thousands of years ago, and never were recorded. Through their vivid imaginations they have been able to re-create for us events and happenings that can make them as real as if we had seen them ourselves. Of course not all their paintings are equally successful. In Liverpool's Walker Art

19 Devil with Hand
clutching a Female
Head. *Hokusai
(1760–1849)
Hokusai mainly painted
landscapes, but he,
like other Japanese
artists, enjoyed
painting devils and
ghosts and monsters.*

21 Dancing Skeletons. *Edward Burra (1905–   )*
Burra has a very vivid imagination. This is a sort of comic nightmare. These four crazy skeletons seem to be having a high old time. You can almost hear their bones rattle and crack in a spanking ghostly rhythm. Notice how the whites sparkle and seem almost to explode against the darks.

20 *(opposite)* The Arming of the Knights. *Tapestry by Sir Edward Burne-Jones (1833–98) (Birmingham Museum and Art Gallery) Edward Burne-Jones, his head always full of fantasies and tales of medieval Knights and their adventures, has made an interesting composition of the ladies and their vertical draperies, the horses' curved necks and rumps and the grouped heads of the Knights.*

Gallery there are two versions of the *Death of Nelson*, by two Victorian painters, Daniel Maclise RA and Benjamin West PRA, both versions of an event that neither actually saw. But one of them is, to my mind, a much more successful picture than the other. If you live in or near Liverpool, go and look at these for yourselves and decide which one *you* like best.

One of the most beautiful and wonderful paintings I have ever seen is a *Nativity* — the birth of Jesus — by an Italian artist called Piero della Francesca, which is in the National Gallery in London. It is full of both realities: the reality of the little Italian town in the background and the imagined reality of the miraculous birth. The shepherds are as earthy and real as any you would see today in the fields; and the grave and lovely angels in their varied blue gowns, standing before the infant lying on the ground are like a song sung in harmony. There are other paintings

22 The Nativity. *Piero della Francesca (1410/20–92)*

of the same subject in that gallery. See if you can find one you like better.

It is through the liveliness and power of the artists' imagination and the depth of their feeling about what they are painting, that they can create whole new worlds for us to inhabit, provided we open our hearts to feel and our eyes to look.

23 Horse frightened by a Lion. *George Stubbs (1724–1806) Stubbs seems to have been haunted by an incident he witnessed in North Africa when a lion attacked a horse, and he made many paintings of this theme. Why does this one make such an exciting picture?*

Science and art

We often think that science and art have nothing to do with each other. We would be wrong, but it seems like this today. During the last few centuries so much has been discovered in so many different aspects of science, that its original connection with art seems to have got completely lost.

Science means knowledge — knowledge gained by careful observation of the world around us — and tested experiment. It can tell us, for instance, how one plant differs from another and how they can be grouped in families. It can tell us the differences and properties of metals and gases, why winds blow or a rainbow appears; it helps to find the origins of diseases and how to find cures for them. Men are everlastingly curious and many have devoted their whole lives to finding out what substances are made of, and how and why things happen. Television, radar and space flights are only a very few of

24 The Monkey. *George Stubbs (1724–1806) Although Stubbs was famous for his paintings of horses, he painted many other animals too. The painting of this little monkey is so beautiful, so sympathetic that one can see that Stubbs loved all animals.*

thousands of projects that are the result of curiosity and scientific research and experiment.

Art is a very difficult word to define. No one has done it quite satisfactorily yet. It really means human skill in making something beautiful or exciting, out of materials that in themselves are neither.

When man first discovered that he could make a design or picture by putting colours and lines down on to a hard surface, he was inventing something. The shapes and lines that he drew came out of himself, out of his own ideas, feelings and imagination. He made a pattern. It was a kind of magic, for out of two quite ordinary substances he made a completely new thing. This new thing could be looked at and enjoyed by others as well as himself.

He found that his eyes and his memory helped him. He observed those things around him that seemed of great importance and he could carry them in his memory. He practised his skills until his hands could perform what his mind told him to do. It is like practising for any game — football, tennis or hockey — you go on and on till you feel confident that your eyes, arms and legs will perform well.

The scientist needs imagination to find the answers to his problems: the artist needs knowledge to obtain the purest, the best and the most suitable materials for his work. Actually, art and science are not so far apart at all, they complement each other. They are like two sides of the same coin. To split the coin in half would be to destroy its value.

The scientist often uses the artist to record his work: his research and eventually his discoveries, particularly for teaching purposes. The surgeon must study anatomy and needs drawings of bones, muscles and nerves. The camera can help a lot, but for the most accurate details, drawings are still necessary. Some of these drawings are so splendid one can call them works of art.

It is the *way* a thing is done that can make it a work of art. In the past many artists were scientists too. George Stubbs, one of our great English painters, was a famous anatomist. He drew,

25 A Camel. *Hendrick Goltzius (1558–1617) This fine, sympathetic drawing of a camel is by a Dutch artist from Haarlem. He probably painted this from a camel in a private zoo.*

engraved and annotated the complete *Anatomy of the Horse* (some of these beautiful drawings can be seen at the Royal Academy Library in London), as well as painting lovely pictures of horses, other animals, landscapes and people (go and look at some at the Walker Art Gallery in Liverpool). John James Audubon was an ornithologist, a man who studies birds, as well as one of the greatest painters of birds. Leonardo da Vinci, who painted the *Mona Lisa*, invented a flying machine and many new forms of weapons. Uccello, another Italian painter, discovered the laws of perspective.

One day a lady was walking down the street and in the window of a shop she saw a hat made of ribbons. It was very pretty. 'Oh,' she thought, 'how well that would go with my new spring suit.' She walked into the shop, and the milliner came out from the back.
'Can I help you?' he said.

'Yes, I should like to see the little hat in the window, made of ribbon.'

'Certainly,' said the man, and drew it out for her to try on. She looked gorgeous in it: it suited her to perfection.

'It is very pretty and does, I think, look well on me.'

'Yes,' said the milliner, walking round her and eyeing her from every side, 'it is quite perfect on you.'

'How much is it?'

'It costs £50, madam.'

'What,' cried the lady in a rage, '£50 for a few little bits of ribbon.'

'Ah,' said the creator of the hat, taking it gently off her head. 'I should be delighted to give you the ribbon free of charge' — and he began to dismantle the enchanting hat — 'perhaps you can make it up yourself.'

4   Colour and drawing

Colour pleasing to the eye

Artists use colour in two ways

Why colour is not used in this book

What is a drawing?

Colour, of course, plays the most important part in painting. It gives a very special pleasure. We enjoy it in nature — we see it in sunsets, in flowers, in trees (how many different shades of green and brown there are!) — we see it in animals and fish. Have you ever noticed that the coloured patterns on butterflies' wings look as if they have been most carefully designed for the wing shape?

Uses of colour

But when artists use colour for a picture they also use it to make a point. It may suggest the atmosphere or mood, or it may describe actual things — a blue book or a pink tablecloth, or it may be used to give the effect of light or distance. Have you ever noticed, for instance, that in sunlight, shadows on snow are light blue, even purple sometimes? Even in ordinary weather, sunny or not, but especially in sun, shadows vary in colour during the day. In the afternoon they are quite different from the morning.

Nobody noticed this much until the Impressionists discovered it. The Impressionists were a group of French nineteenth-century artists, each of whom in his own way discovered that shadows as well as light could be described in colour, not just in tones of brown or grey, and that the warm colours, reds, oranges, yellows and buffs could be used for light, and cool colours, blues and greens and mauves could describe the shadow.

The Tate Gallery and the National Gallery and the Courtauld Gallery in London; the Welsh National Gallery in Cardiff; the Art Gallery in Glasgow and the National Gallery in Edinburgh are among the places where Impressionist pictures of landscapes, figure compositions and portraits can be seen. Go and look at them. I am sure you will enjoy them, they are so full of colour and light.

Then go and compare them with some paintings of the same sort of subjects made about a hundred years earlier — in the late eighteenth century — paintings by Reynolds or Gainsborough, Crome or Wilson. Make no mistake, all these artists painted splendid pictures too, but they do look much darker than the later ones. The earlier painters used colour in a quite different and much more sober way. It was really the scientists in the nineteenth century, with their research into the nature of light and colour, who influenced the artists. Their discoveries were published in books and journals and there was a lot of discussion about their theories. Artists began looking at nature and the objects around them with a new eye, and discovered that light and shadow could be described in colours rather than the tones between black and white.

Colour too can be used for its own sake — a pattern of colour relationships can be both exciting and beautiful. The very early

26 View at Auvers. *Vincent van Gogh (1853–90) Van Gogh was one of the greatest modern painters. This painting is of a pretty village in Northern France where he came to consult a doctor, whose understanding of artists was famous. See what you can discover about van Gogh's life.*

27 Snowdon. Richard Wilson (1713–82) Richard Wilson was called the father of English landscape painting because he was the first English artist to paint landscape for its own sake. Here it is not the group of fishermen in the foreground that he was particularly interested in, but the nobility of the Welsh mountains. See how the darkened middleground and the scoop of the rock pinpoints the peak of Snowdon.

painters in Europe, in the thirteenth, fourteenth or fifteenth centuries used far fewer colours than we do now, because they had not yet been invented, but those they did use were very pure and brilliant. They have lovely decorative, jewel-like effects, as they were used almost flat, without any attempt at modelling at all. Painting varies from century to century and each period has its own particular interest and charm.

Why colour is not used in this book

Are you surprised that there are no pictures in colour in this book? I wonder if you can guess why.

Well, there are two good reasons. First, because to reproduce colour well is very expensive indeed. It is not so expensive when the pictures are made especially for the book: then the illustrator can limit his colours as much as he likes; also there are methods of printing flat colour that are reasonably cheap. But when you have to reproduce a painting that was made only to be seen in the original, then the processes are very difficult and subtle and need a lot of care. To reproduce a variety of paintings in colour would make the cost of this book so high that only a very few people could afford to buy it.

But there is a second reason and very important it is too. However near in reproduction the colour might be, it could never be quite the same as the original. More often than not, the picture would have to be considerably reduced in size for reproduction and the effect would be quite different.

When I was fourteen years old I bought a reproduction of Fra Angelico's painting called the *Annunciation*. It was quite small but I thought it very pretty. But when, later, I saw the real picture in Florence, I had a tremendous surprise. It was enormous, and it was not *pretty* at all: it had grandeur; it was marvellous and unforgettable. And I realised when I looked at the painting that I wasn't only enjoying the subject but was also learning a lot about the artist as well: about his devotion and his feeling of wonder at the miraculous happening.

Every picture shown in this book can be found in one of our own museums or art galleries. So if you like the look of any of the reproductions, you can go and discover what the picture really looks like. See for yourself how the colour and the size affects the whole thing. Make up your own mind about it.

Drawing
Before I go on to the next chapter, I should like to tell you a little about drawing. Most people think of pictures as being primarily in colour, and so they are. But, all over the world, and at all times people have made drawings as touching, as thrilling and beautiful as paintings. Sometimes a little colour is used in a drawing, but not often. A little girl talking of her drawing once said: 'I think, and then I put a line round my think.'

Line can be of any kind: thin, tough, wiry, heavy, thick, soft, flowing, scratchy or uneven. It can describe an object in great

28 Orchestra on Stage *(drawing in Chinese ink). Edmond X. Kapp (1890–   )*
You can almost hear the music coming from this orchestra. The drawing is so simple, so true, yet there is no detail, no description. The blacks of the lampshades and of the men's suits and the instruments, the podium and the conductor's expressive figure, make a dark oval in which the light and the sound is concentrated.

detail or suggest it with a single stroke. A fine drawing can be a source of pure delight. In my opinion good drawing is the basis of all good art: it is like the bony skeleton of a body, displaying the structure and underlying shape of what is sometimes a highly complicated object. Even abstract drawings — drawings that do not describe any particular thing — can produce a mood or emotion, they can even be funny. Joan Miró, a Spanish painter, has sometimes made pictures of line and mass that can make one chuckle. The joy that a good drawing can give lies often in the spareness, strength and suppleness of the line.

Both the Chinese and Japanese practised drawing as they practised handwriting and both nations have produced wonderful drawings. To be able to draw and to write well was the sign of a well-educated person.

鐵
嶺
高
其
佩

29 Man with Umbrella
in the Snow *(Chinese
finger-tip painting).
Kao Ch'i-p'ei (1672–
1734)*

30 Woman's Head.
Edmond X. Kapp
(1890–   )

Leonardo da Vinci tried to draw everything he saw, from a seed or a muscle to the swirling waters of a river in spate. Holbein could, by a very few marks on paper, create a calm, shrewd face or a complicated dubious character. Rembrandt, one of the greatest of them all, could bring the movements of a huge seething crowd, the tenderness of a mother with her baby, or a lively girl twisting to look out of a window, with a few touches of the brush or pen on to a sheet of paper with such masterliness that we can feel sheer delight.

The greatest draughtsman of our own time was Picasso. His drawings are superb. He tackled everything: men, women, children, imaginary beasts and real animals, tense bullfights, graceful dancers, acrobats, horses and their riders, in fact any subject you can think of. His drawings have such splendid swinging rhythms that they are a joy to look at.

So when you are looking at paintings, don't forget to look at drawings too. They can give you a lot of pleasure. Look at the drawing opposite of an old lady. You can see that she's not an ordinary person at all, can't you? How would you describe her character from what the drawing tells you? Note how different the Chinese drawing of an old man is from the other, yet they have certain things in common. What do you think they are?

5   Portraits and occasions

Variety in people's looks

Painting and photography

Recording both great and small occasions

It is strange, isn't it, that though everybody has two eyes, a nose, a mouth and a couple of ears, they should look so different from each other. Identical twins are often very difficult to tell apart, but if we look carefully enough we will be bound to find some small difference; one of them may be a tiny bit taller than the other, or perhaps a little fairer.

31 The Graham Children. *William Hogarth (1697–1764) It is difficult to believe that children in the eighteenth century wore clothes like this to play in. They are very pretty but they are all dressed like their elders, even the two-year-old. Why do you think this was so?*

32 Self-portrait. *Rembrandt van Rijn (1606–69) This is one of the very greatest of Rembrandt's self-portraits. Here he is in ripe middle age; wise, compassionate and understanding, and he does not try to hide his faults. And how beautifully and naturally the head is placed on the canvas against the pale background with those faint ovals, giving a feeling of infinity.*

Variety in people's looks

It is only since people began to take a scientific interest in nature itself, that they showed real curiosity about what they looked like and that they realised that we all are very different from each other. The harder they looked the more variety they noticed.

Gradually they realised that physical features like a big nose or a long neck, can be handed down from parents to children (even from uncles and aunts or grandparents), so that the members of one family very often resemble each other. They also came to notice that character and personality, even occupation some-

33 Portrait of a Lady in Yellow. *Alessio Baldovinetti (c. 1545–99)*
It is not usual to paint a portrait in profile, but here the whole picture
conveys an impression of calmness and inwardness as well as creating a
lovely pattern against the dark background.

times, can give the face and even the body, subtle variations in shape and line.

At first portraits were only painted for special occasions and of special people, kings and queens, nobles and other great men or women. The Copts (a Christian sect who live in Egypt) used, in the past, to paint portraits on coffin lids to show who lay within, but even here likenesses were very superficial. You can see some of these coffin lids in the British Museum and other museums.

Often the aim of the portrait was to make people look impressive and splendid, not to show people as they really were. When travel was extremely arduous and difficult, portraits of princes and princesses used to be sent to their prospective wives or husbands so that they could get some idea of what they looked like. Often they received a great shock when they actually met.

34 Robin. *Augustus John (1878–1961) How different this portrait is from the last! Here a tempestuous boy with a wilful character, but with eyes of indisputable honesty, looks out at you. It is obviously a painting of today.*

Painting and photography

Since the invention of the camera, photography has, to a great extent, taken the place of painted portraits and nowadays there are not nearly as many portrait painters as there used to be. If you go into your local Town Hall, maybe you will find a few painted portraits of past Mayors or Lord Mayors and quite a few framed photographs of later ones. Which do you like best?

Probably the painted portraits are not very good, but personally I always find I enjoy the painted ones more than the photographs, which usually look rather faded, dreary and dull.

A good portrait painted by a perceptive artist can tell us a great deal about his sitter, much more sometimes than a written description. Something we see with our eyes penetrates our minds more quickly and more deeply. Just like the road signs we have talked about: pictures can tell us a great deal almost immediately.

Have you yourself noticed how very varied the human face is? One eye is sometimes a little larger than the other; ears can be coarse or delicate; foreheads high or low; but mouths and the expression round them are the most meaningful of all features. They are more indicative of character and personality than the rest of the face. Eyes can be beautiful and expressive, but they can lie; whereas the shape of the mouth and the tiny fine lines round it are things that develop gradually and cannot lie.

Without staring or being rude, go and observe people for yourself. Notice the shape of the back of the head and the cheek bones. Is the jaw rounded or square? Do eyebrows beetle over the nose or ride high and arched above the eyes? Do lips curve up or down? What about the hair, is it straight and sleek or curly and vigorous? Notice how the head fits on to the neck and the neck on to the body; does it poke forward or hold itself straight? Do eyes sparkle and shine or are they dull, and are there tiny lines fanning out from the corners of the eyes? How much there is to notice in a head!

Of course babies' faces don't have the variety that is found in grown-ups, but even they vary quite a bit. Try and make a portrait yourself, of your father or mother or a friend and see how

35 The Countess of Howe. *Thomas Gainsborough (1727–88)*
This is one of Gainsborough's loveliest portraits. It is all in pinks and greys.
Consider the pose: it is quite tranquil, but the fluttery laces and silks give a
feeling of movement – of a pleasant walk interrupted for a moment.

36 Mr and Mrs Atherton.
Arthur Devis
(1711–87)
Notice three things
about this picture: the
charm and clarity of
the composition, the
uncluttered look of
this eighteenth-century
room and the lack of
carpet and curtains;
even quite large houses
before about 1780
rarely had these.

successful you can be in giving it the character you think belongs to the original. Even if you are not particularly clever in mixing paints, it does not matter. You might see something in your subject that nobody has noticed before — and produce an interesting portrait.

In the National Portrait Gallery in London there are hundreds of paintings and drawings of all sorts of famous people. Go and look for yourself and see if you can find a portrait of your favourite character there. Maybe you will see a number of portraits of the same person by different artists. Do these versions vary much? Perhaps one artist has found something in his sitter that the other did not notice. A famous artist once said: there should be a touch of caricature in all portraits. Do you think he was right?

Recording important occasions

When we go on holiday, or there is to be a wedding or a christening in the family, the first thing we all want is a camera so that we can take photographs of the event. We want to remember the pleasure and fun we have had, the funny times and the grave ones. Later, we look at those snaps and they can bring back the oddest, merriest moments. Even if the occasion is very grand like a coronation, or the visit of an astronaut or Cup-Tie winning team, or the arrival of a famous dancer or pop-singer, out come the cameras and we click away like mad, hoping to catch the excitement so that, later on, we can enjoy it all over again. But photographs are apt to fade in time. Perhaps when our grandsons and granddaughters come to look at these souvenirs of the past, they may find them faint and barely recognisable.

37 The Last of England. *Ford Madox Brown (1821–93) (Birmingham Museum and Art Gallery) Here are English emigrants. I wonder if you could make up a story about this sad and resentful young couple, who are leaving their native shores for ever.*

There was a time of course, when cameras did not exist. Yet we have some superb records of every conceivable sort of happening and occasion from the past, some grand, some intimate and these were painted by the artists of the time. There were pageants and regattas, coronations and betrothals. There were battles and the return of victorious armies with loot and prisoners. There were religious or festive processions, visits of ambassadors. There were parties, wrestling or boxing matches, concerts and plays and a hundred other splendid occasions.

38 Work. *Ford Madox Brown (1821–93)*
A great deal is going on in this picture and as it is a bit muddly, you need to look at it rather carefully. See if you can tell what story it tells. The two men leaning against the railing, talking and watching, are Thomas Carlyle the famous historian, in the hat, and F. D. Maurice, founder of the Working Men's College, holding a book.

39 Regatta on the
Grand Canal, Venice.
*Antonio Canaletto
(1697–1768)
Venice, in the
eighteenth century,
was famous for its
carnivals, festivals and
balls. Because of its
splendid canals, a
favourite form of
entertainment was the
regatta.*

40 La Plage (The Beach). *Edgar Degas (1834–1917)*
*Degas has caught both the feeling and the whole lazy atmosphere of an
unfrequented beach. If you trace an imaginary line from the girl's feet, along
the top of the sunshade and the nurse's head and down to the top of the bag
with the towel hanging out of it, you will have described a great arc and
within that is concentrated the main story of the picture. What else is happening? One group, swathed in towels, is walking straight out of the picture.
This was a new idea. No one had dared to do that before this period. But how
natural and normal it looks. The black bag on the right and the white hat on
the left hold the composition firmly in place.*

41 Indians of
Virginia fishing.
John White
This artist accompanied
one of the first
expeditions to America
in the sixteenth
century.

Had we not these paintings to look at we should know much less of the past. They tell us a lot of fascinating things: about the splendour of great occasions or the charm of intimate ones; about the clothes that were worn by the rich and the poor; about the armour, weapons, ships, flags and standards, sport, animals, carriages and carts, food and drink and furniture and many other things besides.

Then there were the expeditions that went on long journeys of exploration into unknown lands, and often with them went an artist to record the landscapes of the new countries and the strange people they saw, their adventures and discoveries. These paintings are very valuable documents and full of information, as well as being a great source of pleasure.

6 Landscape, decoration and still life

The changing countryside

The Grand Tour and its effects

Universal love of ornament

The fascination of everyday objects

The pleasure that people take in landscape painting is, in England, even more recent than in portraiture. It is not generally known that it was really the artists who first made the countryside popular.

The changing countryside

This is how it happened: in England before the eighteenth century no one bothered much about nature. To most educated

42 Study for The Leaping Horse. *John Constable (1776–1837) (Victoria and Albert Museum. Crown Copyright.)* Constable, unlike painters before him, liked to paint land-scapes when the sun was overhead; mostly landscapes were painted in the afternoon light when the air was golden and objects threw long shadows. But Constable enjoyed the reflected light on leaves and water that danced and sparkled in the sun.

43 Snow Landscape.
*Hiroshige (1797–
1858)*
*Many artists enjoy
painting landscape
under snow. But what
differences can you
find between this
Japanese snowscape
and an English one?
There are at least five.*

people the countryside was a place where people lived hard and brutish lives, growing crops and keeping pigs and cattle. It was one long fight with nature and the weather. It was a continual and bitter struggle just to keep alive with little time for fun and relaxation. Forests and mountains harboured outlaws and brigands.

Royalty and great noblemen had built great fortified castles or grand palaces dotted over the countryside but these were mainly for defence and the display of power and grandeur. Travelling to and from the cities and towns was a tedious and often dangerous affair, and huge retinues of soldiers and courtiers had to accompany their lords and keep marauders at bay. The greater part of the population lived in hovels or rough farmhouses — both equally damp and unhygienic.

But at the end of the Civil War things began to change, to settle down. Trade prospered, new ideas began to spring up and already during the reign of Queen Anne in the early eighteenth century the country was very gradually being transformed. Successful merchants bought land from the impoverished aristocracy, and took to hunting, fishing and shooting for pleasure and not out of necessity. They welcomed new ideas, and gradually the whole pattern of farming changed. Hedges

44 Pegwell Bay.
William Dyce
(1806–64)
Compare this painting
to Degas's picture of
the beach. Which do
you like better?

were planted, new crops grown and new ideas on cattle breed-
ing and crop rotation were put into practice. These brought
great success and prosperity. Merchants ploughed their profits
back into the land, and bit by bit spent less of their time in their
offices and more in the country. They built fine houses, improved the farms, rebuilt whole villages and planned their
estates. Both roads and vehicles improved and it was easier and
more comfortable to get about. Apart from mountains, caves and
moors, the look of the countryside began to change.

The Grand Tour

It became the fashion for gentlemen and their sons to complete
their education by taking what was called the 'Grand Tour' – a
leisurely trip through Europe lasting anything between six
months and three years. They took with them a coach and
coachman, a valet, and sometimes a cook and a 'limner'. A

limner was a man who could draw, and paint in watercolour. He was taken on the journey so that he could record any place that took the fancy of the traveller, as today we would take a camera.

When the traveller returned, his family were shown the collection of drawings and paintings of all the fascinating places he had seen or visited, the fabulous mountains of the Alps, the wide river landscapes of the Netherlands or the beautiful Greek and Roman ruins and landscapes of Italy. Looking at these souvenirs of the voyage became a popular pastime, so engravings and etchings were made of the originals and published in books or folios and sold quite cheaply.

Also the travellers often brought back splendid paintings they had bought in Rome, the city they all aimed to visit — for it was the centre where great painters and sculptors from all over Europe had chosen to live. Many of these paintings were landscapes. British artists noted all this and began going abroad on their own to paint landscapes.

Landscape painting

Soon they began to notice their own country and to realise that it contained beauties, different perhaps, but as fine as could be

45 Hull from the Humber. *John Ward (1798–1849) Notice the neat calm painting of houses and ships and compare it with Constable's landscapes.*

46 Dressed Overall at
the Quay, Port Said.
*Edward Wadsworth
(1889–1949)
What does dressed
overall mean? How
does the picture show
it?*

found abroad. So they began to paint their own mountains and valleys, villages and fields, trees, rivers and bridges. They celebrated the glorious skies of East Anglia, the storm clouds over the mountains of Wales and the Lake District, the tranquil villages and scenery of the rest of Britain.

Gradually the new interest in landscape shown by our native artists and the paintings brought from the Continent, started to make itself felt, and people began to enjoy not only the pictures but the countryside itself. A great and important school of landscape painting grew up in Britain and among the very many who added to its lustre were John Constable, J. M. W. Turner, John Sell Cotman and Thomas Girtin, some of whose work influenced French artists of the nineteenth century.

The Impressionists, that group of great French painters of a later generation, working between 1860 and 1910, learned a lot from our landscape artists. They added town- and city-scapes to their repertoire and with their new feeling for colour we can enjoy them as much as we can the older landscapes.

47 Bridge in Rain. *Hiroshige (1797–1858) This is a Japanese wood-cut. Notice how the signature and title help the design of the picture.*

48 Barges on the
Thames. *André Derain*
(1880–1954)
André Derain was a
member of a group
called the Fauves (the
wild ones) because
they did not copy
nature's colours, but
painted in brilliant hues
that made an exciting
colour composition,
relying on their good
drawing to make the
painting valid.

I wonder if you can find any spots in your own city, town or village, in your park or on the river or canal, that you would like to paint yourself?

In the Tate Gallery and the Victoria and Albert Museum in London you can find superb Turners and Constables. In the Castle Museum in Norwich is a large collection of beautiful Cotmans and at the Whitworth Art Gallery in Manchester and the Leeds City Art Gallery are splendid collections of eighteenth- and nineteenth-century water-colours. Also at all the galleries in London I have already mentioned you can see fine collections of Impressionist paintings.

Ornament and decoration

Almost everybody enjoys ornament and decoration. People did in the past too. Primitive man painted designs on his own body (even today some people enjoy being tattooed). Even guns and cannons, in the past, had beautiful carvings, mouldings and engravings on them. Go and see some in the Tower of London.

In Roman times gay and charming pictures and decorations were painted on the walls of houses, both inside and out. As I have mentioned before, all churches were covered with painting and decoration. Most of it has been destroyed, but if you are near Pickering in North Yorkshire, go and look at the Parish Church, where quite a lot of painting remains, or find the little Church of St Thomas in Salisbury or the Cathedral of St David's in South Wales and see if you can imagine how it must have looked when all the walls and pillars were covered with ornament and pictures.

In London there is a church, St Anselm, in Lambeth, in the Kennington Road, with some large new abstract decorations on the walls, based on the *Pilgrim's Progress*, a book written in prison by John Bunyan. It tells the story of the hero, Christian's, journey through life and all the adventures he had, the good and bad people he met, all the trials and difficulties he had to get through, and how eventually he overcame them. These paintings are, to my mind, very exciting. They were done by Norman Adams. Make an expedition there one day and see what you think of them. Ask the Vicar to talk to you about them. I am sure he will be pleased to do so. Maybe near where you live there are other churches and public buildings, including schools, which have modern decorations. See whether you like them and try and find out who did them.

Today we still enjoy decoration. We like coloured patterns on our clothes; on shirts, dresses, socks, sweaters and ties. We like designs on curtains, cushions, crockery, carpets and wallpaper. We like jewellery and lace. There always was, and still is a great pleasure in pretty and colourful ornament.

Sometimes, in a book, decoration used to be combined with illustration: the picture would illustrate the story and the decoration would be painted round the edge of the page, just to give pleasure to the eye. Many of these 'illuminated' books, as we call them, can be seen in the British Museum in London and in museums in other parts of the country. Even musical scores used to be decorated in the same way. How do you think our comic and strip cartoons compare with these?

49 St Elizabeth of
Hungary. *Miniature
from a Book of Hours.
(c. 1480)
A 'Book of Hours' is a
series of religious or
devotional texts
illustrated by minia-
tures. It is called an
'Hours' because it is
subdivided into eight
parts, one for each of
the liturgical hours of
the day. Notice how
the illustration is
surrounded by a pretty
border of flowers.*

Everyday objects

Long ago artists sometimes put a vase of flowers or a dish of fruit
into a picture, just as decoration, but it never occurred to
them that these things were worth painting for their own sake.
But for quite a long time now artists have found interest and
pleasure in painting the most ordinary and familiar things of
everyday life. Flowers, plants, a plate of shining fish, pots and
pans, musical instruments, vegetables, fruit — all seem to satisfy
a real passion for shape and texture as well as colour.

Many seventeenth-century Dutch artists delighted in their new,
clean, well-lit houses with their uncluttered rooms and their
bright household utensils, the sun slanting in, making patterns
of light and shade on the white walls. They also had a passion
for flowers, fruit and game and they painted these everyday
things with the greatest love and skill.

50 Still Life with Apples and Pomegranate. *Gustave Courbet (1819–77)* Would you not like to take up one of these apples and munch it? There is such richness and joy in the fruit itself that it is quite difficult not to want to do this. Why do you think the artist has put the one pomegranate to nestle among all those apples?

51 Still Life. *A follower of Jean-Baptiste-Simeon Chardin (eighteenth century)* Until recently this painting was considered to be by Chardin himself. Scientific research has discovered it is not. Nevertheless it is a lovely painting. Go and see it for yourself.

No one would ever think that a pair of old boots could provide a subject for a picture. Vincent van Gogh did, however; and so deeply did he feel about these old boots that he painted two or

52 Poultry. Aelbert Cuyp (1620–91) Aelbert Cuyp (pronounced Kipe) was a great Dutch painter who took enormous pleasure in all aspects of the countryside. Notice how the heads of the sitting birds fit into the curve of the standing hen's breast and neck. These ordinary birds, the artist is saying, have lovely plumage and are as much part of the life of the country as the church in the background and the farmhouse on the left.

three versions of them. He seems to be telling us the whole story of some labourer's hard and painful life. Though the boots themselves may be old and unlovely, shapeless and cracked, it is *the way* they are painted that shows us all the compassion, love and pity van Gogh felt for suffering and hardworking mankind. Don't think he could not paint happy pictures too. He did. Paintings of great sunflowers, irises and peonies, glorious landscapes and gay interiors. You can tell, just by looking at them, how much he loved life. When the French artists, Courbet or Cézanne painted apples, you feel how good a bite of these would be. They are the very essence of apple, though they are very different from each other. I wonder if you can find some paintings of still life that make you feel that the artist loved the things he painted so much that he has been able to make you see these things with new eyes.

Fun, games, caricature and cartoon

Pleasure in games, dancing and sport

Caricature and cartoon

We all enjoy playing games of one sort or another. When we are little, we hop, skip or jump about, sometimes playing old and well-known games, sometimes inventing new ones of our own.

Games
As we grow older we enjoy playing organised games: football, tennis, hockey, cricket, among others. We may play snakes and ladders, draughts, scrabble, chess and all sorts of card games; we enjoy boxing, wrestling and fencing. Artists have sometimes made fascinating pictures of these activities. Have you ever been to a circus and watched trapeze artistes and acrobats, and those wonderful horse-back riders who perform superb feats of balance and horsemanship as the horses gallop round the ring? Are you surprised that artists have wanted to paint pictures of these subjects?

Dancing
Dancers too, have always fascinated artists. Their movements are so graceful and the shapes and patterns their bodies describe in the air as well as on the ground, are so enchanting, that from the earliest times, artists have tried to interpret their lovely and intricate movements in their own way. Edgar Degas, a French Impressionist painter, enjoyed drawing ballet dancers in action and also when resting or practising.

I wonder how many pictures of dancers you can find — on Greek pots or Cretan frescoes or Egyptian tombs and elsewhere. You may find it difficult to see the real ones, but there are always books with good illustrations to look at.

53 Detail from a hand-scroll, The Hundred Children, *in ink and colours on silk. Chinese, seventeenth century. It is called 'Music and Acrobatics'. This is a charming painting, with the great gnarled tree and its delicate foliage making a framework for the boys' activities. What are they all doing?*

54 Detail from a hand-scroll, The Hundred Children, The Puppet Play. *Chinese, seventeenth century. There are a lot of things to be noticed in this picture. First that Chinese boys three hundred years ago had their hair cut in a very different way from nowadays. Their clothes too were very different. But one thing is the same. All of them are quite absorbed, and enjoying what they are doing.*

At Wakefield City Art Gallery, there's a picture of a cricket match; it's a sunny, hot, lazy sort of picture. Is it like your idea of a cricket match or not?

Caricatures

Sometimes, we all like poking fun at people, especially those who are pompous, cantankerous, toffee-nosed, cruel or mean; or over-rowdy, drunk, noisy or disorderly — or just very silly.

Hogarth and Rowlandson in the eighteenth century in England and Daumier and Gavarni in the nineteenth in France are only four among hundreds and hundreds of caricaturists and cartoonists who enjoyed poking fun at people in paintings and drawings, at the vulgar, greedy, vain, unjust or conceited.

A caricature is a drawing that emphasises and mocks at both the physical features and moral weaknesses of men and women.

55 The French Hunt *Thomas Rowlandson (1756–1827) You can see for yourself what Rowlandson thought of French huntsmen. What a mess they have got themselves into! One can almost sense the stag laughing at them.*

56 Philip Wilson Steer.
*Max Beerbohm
(1872–1956)
(Ashmolean Museum,
Oxford)*
Can you read the
original caption? Use a
magnifying glass if the
writing is too small for
you to read easily. This
caricature of a well-
known English painter
is witty but not cruel.

A cartoon is a picture of ideas, that ridicules the stupidity or injustice of a political situation or a social custom.

Caricaturists and cartoonists have helped to make people aware of the faults and foibles of those in high and important places, and of the social and political evils of their period.

Cartoons

Thomas Rowlandson was a splendid draughtsman; he could draw the most delightful and lively pictures of people and landscape. But he could also make strong and biting comments on the social conditions of his time: on drunkenness, on the stupidity of dress or habit, on injustice and so on. His coloured drawings and prints (some very harsh indeed) are as enjoyable today as they were in his own time.

Thomas Gillray was another splendid draughtsman and his cartoons on the political events of his day were vigorous and stinging. Both these artists tell us a lot about their own period, which was the late eighteenth and early nineteenth centuries. They were the best out of very many other cartoonists and caricaturists of their time.

Nearer our own day, Max Beerbohm (who was also a writer), was a very good and funny cartoonist and caricaturist. His work is most enjoyable and sometimes very funny. One of our best living cartoonists is Giles, of the *Daily Express*. He has a very funny style and is often well worth looking at.

8   Time and change: modern painting

When life changes, art changes

The artist's dual job

Style

New ways of seeing and expressing

When life changes, art changes
There are revolutions in art as there are in life. In life they occur when, in any one place, conditions of living become unbearable. Revolutions in art are bloodless, building up gradually and are the result of new ideas trying to push out old and outworn ones.

The only difference between artists and other people is that they have the capacity to express themselves in a way that moves us. We can all be sensitive and understanding but only a few of us have the particular talent needed to express our feelings and ideas really well, whether it be in writing, music or painting.

The artist's dual job
The artist's job is a dual one. Through his imagination and feeling he can make us more aware, more alive to all that is going on around us: not only the beauty and excitement, but also the ugliness, dishonesty and distress, that exists in the world. His other job is to design the objects we use — but it is in his first capacity we are considering him now.

When the subjects that artists paint become repetitive, empty, silly, sentimental or pompous, their art no longer has the ability to move us: it becomes insipid and dead.

This is felt strongly by young artists today who feel a new spirit in life and are revolting against outworn and overworked ideas.

57 Vertical Seconds.
*Ben Nicholson
(1894–)
The artist has
invented a pattern
made up of the shapes
of parts of goblets and
bottles, the whole
welded together by
fine hard lines and
patches of colour. He
does not describe the
objects he uses, he is
just making a fascina-
ting design in which
your eye can take an
imaginary walk.*

58 Woman, Bird by Moonlight. *Joan Miró (1893–   ). (©) by A.D.A.G.P., Paris, 1974)*
All sorts of exciting things are happening in this picture. Miró has invented shapes and lines, and they all seem to be moving about in a night sky, the blacks and whites making a play against each other. It is strange that without telling any story, Miró can give you such a strong feeling of mystery, fun and adventure. Do you get it too?

The world we live in has changed more in the last seventy years than in hundreds of years before. The changes have come very quickly and are mainly due to the development of science. When everything else changes, is it surprising that art changes too? Artists have reacted to these changes and have produced not one sort of new painting but very many different kinds.

It is all a bit difficult to keep up with, but if we remain unprejudiced, and go on looking hard, we will soon find things we like and can enjoy.

Style
What we call style is the unique way in which each artist makes
his marks on paper or canvas (or in whatever medium he works).
We can say of a person, 'I like her style of dressing', or 'that
man has style', meaning that the way that particular man acts,
the way he walks, talks, dresses and behaves generally has a
personal flavour and is unlike anyone else. You will recognise
him at once by his style. You can have style in everything you do,
in driving a car or in riding a horse, or playing football or tennis.

Style in painting comes from inside yourself; it is not something
you consciously create, it is gradually formed by your whole
personality. An artist may have more than one style during a
lifetime of work. As he grows older he may change. He develops
new thoughts and ideas and has to find new ways of expressing
them. This will create a new style.

Often when people are working close together, when their
feelings and thoughts are similar, their styles may be similar
too. But the more mature they grow, the more they will develop
their own individual style.

New ways of seeing and expressing
In the last quarter of the nineteenth century the Impressionists
and then the Post-Impressionists were producing paintings
which we today find completely delightful, though at the time
they were painted the manner of the painting seemed to most
people outrageous. These painters, Pissarro, Manet, Monet,
Renoir, van Gogh, Gauguin, Cézanne, just to mention a few, were
hated and ridiculed while they lived. They could hardly make a
living. Now, we find no difficulty at all in looking at and enjoying
their work, Painters of the early twentieth century like Picasso,
Matisse, Bracque and Rouault in France and Wyndham Lewis,
Paul Nash, William Roberts and Ben Nicholson in England who
have seen familiar and everyday things in completely new ways,
have created exciting and new beauties for us, just as the
inventors of aeroplanes have done.

They paint and draw in the way they do because of their highly

59 Spiral Motif.
Victor Pasmore
(1908–   )
Pasmore has obviously been observing a pool set between rocks; but instead of painting the scene realistically, he has preferred to make a sort of abstract of it. He has traced the lines of the water as it flows here and there and eddies in spirals.

inventive talents, their strong feelings and their reaction to the world around them.

We are all part of this period and sometimes we find their pictures more meaningful, more valid and exciting than older ones. They speak our language and interpret our dreams.

But all art, if it is honest and not bogus, can speak to us. Because although ideas and the mechanics of life change, there are basic feelings and happenings that do not. Birth and death, love and wonder, honour and happiness, as well as hate,

60 Taïmyr. *Victor Vaserely (1908–   ). (© by S.P.A.D.E.M., Paris, 1974)*
I have no idea what the title means. To me this abstract picture has no meaning but itself. You can enjoy it nevertheless, just as you can enjoy a tree. That too has no meaning but itself. The pattern is intricate. From the small flat circular disc in the centre of the picture, the diamond, vertical, horizontal and diagonal patterns seem to fall naturally into the four quarters of the design.

fear, greed and malice, all have remained the same since the beginning of time. Art through all ages has always expressed these, and many other things as well, in one form or another and if we keep our eyes, minds and hearts open, we can respond to and enjoy the painters of our own time.

There have been many new movements in art in the last seventy years. After the turn of the century there came Cubism and the Fauves in France, Futurism in Italy, de Stijl in Holland, Vorticism in England, Expressionism in Germany, Dadaism in Switzerland and many others. Most of these movements have died out, but all had an enormous general influence, not only on art, but on life itself. The feeling for pure, bright colours we enjoy so much today in our house-decoration or clothes is the direct result of the brilliant colours used by many of the new artists. The painters of 'abstract pictures' — paintings in which there are no recognisable things like people, houses or trees but are made up of a sort of pattern of shapes, colours and lines — have given us new ideas on the exterior and interior designs of buildings and even the planning of towns.

These new kinds of paintings can be very exciting and beautiful. Go and look at some at the Tate Gallery in London, the Gallery of Modern Art in Edinburgh, the Art Galleries in Glasgow, Birmingham, Liverpool, Sheffield, Manchester, Leeds and Hull, where you can see both modern painting and sculpture. It is a journey of real adventure to enter a gallery of modern art. The essence of all adventure is discovery. What you may discover depends a great deal on yourself. The bolder and more imaginative you are, the greater and more thrilling the finds. If you can enjoy at least some of what you see, you will be enriching yourself.

What do we gain by enjoying pictures?

9

Spontaneous and thoughtful enjoyment

Developing a critical faculty

Exploring the mind and sense of sight

I ended the last chapter by saying that we enrich ourselves by enjoying paintings. First, we can widen our field of pleasure; and second, we train our mind and observation to be more acute, although we do not know we are doing this.

Enjoyment

Sometimes we can see a painting and immediately and spontaneously enjoy it. But it is difficult to get complete pleasure from what we see and to appreciate a work of art fully, in the same way as we can enjoy the scent of a flower or the taste of food. Some effort on our part, some attempt to put ourselves into the artist's skin is necessary for full enjoyment. We need to use the mind as well as the eye and the imagination to get everything we can out of a picture. But once we start really looking, little by little, this can all come.

The critical faculty

There are so many things we can take pleasure in. Friends and music and sport are just a few; painting, if we can enjoy it, is something for all our lives — the more we look the more interested we can get and the more we can enjoy. Gradually we come to notice all sorts of things we have never noticed before. The composition of one picture seems to be utterly successful, of another it seems a failure; we begin to wonder why.

Our eyes and minds are opened to all sorts of new thoughts

and ideas. We widen our experience. We can develop a critical faculty about shape and colour and line and space and texture. Everything around us, everything we use, is made of these qualities — houses and streets, furniture and light fittings, carpets and crockery — all are made up of shape, colour, line and texture. The feeling for space and proportion too can help us understand why we like one building or bridge or street lamp and not another.

The ability to choose the better thing rather than the less good begins to grow. And how important that is, for we are always having to make choices, all through our lives. The feeling and understanding we have gained through our eyes, through looking at and absorbing and enjoying painting, will help us all to make good choices. Maybe we shall become town councillors or members of Parliament and how important these choices will be then.

As we are all different from each other, thank heaven, we will make different choices; but if we know how to look clearly we will not be taken in, or cheated by pretentiousness, by vulgarity or fake.

Exploring the mind

Most of us like to explore, we enjoy finding new places, new caves, new roads or paths, new towns or cities, new people, new aspects of the world around us. But we can explore our own minds too. Exploring what lies within us is just as exciting and surprising as exploring what lies outside. And what is so important is that it can go on all our lives. Physical muscles grow weaker and stiffer as we grow older, but mental muscles can get stronger and even more flexible as time goes on. So long as we use them, so long as we stretch and exercise them and keep them alert and fit. This means that the older we grow the more we can experience and enjoy. Is this not enriching ourselves?

10

Some of the principal art galleries in Britain

Aberdeen	Art Gallery and Museum, Schoolhill
Barnard Castle	The Bowes Museum
Bath	The Holburne of Menstrie Museum, Great Pulteney Street
Belfast	Ulster Museum, Botanic Gardens
Birkenhead	Williamson Art Gallery and Museum, Slatey Road
Birmingham	City Museum and Art Gallery, Congreve Street
Bradford	City Art Gallery and Museum, Cartwright Hall
Brighton	Museum and Art Gallery and the Royal Pavilion, North Gate House, Church Street
Bristol	City Art Gallery, Queen's Road
Cambridge	Fitzwilliam Museum, Trumpington Street
Cardiff	The National Museum of Wales, Cathays Park
Dundee	City Museum and Art Gallery, Albert Square
Durham	Gulbenkian Museum of Oriental Art and Archeology, The University
Edinburgh	National Gallery of Scotland, The Mound
	Scottish National Portrait Gallery, Queen Street
	Scottish National Gallery of Modern Art, Inverleith House, Royal Botanic Gardens
Glasgow	Art Gallery and Museum, Kelvin Grove
	The Hunterian Museum, University of Glasgow

Ipswich	The Museum, High Street
	Christchurch Mansion, Christchurch Park
Kingston-upon-Hull	Ferens Art Gallery, Queen Victoria Square
Leeds	City Art Gallery, The Headrow
	Temple Newsam House
Leicester	Museum and Art Gallery, New Walk
Liverpool	Walker Art Gallery
London	British Museum
	The Queen's Gallery, Buckingham Palace
	Courtauld Institute Galleries, Woburn Square
	Dulwich College Picture Gallery, College Road, Dulwich
	Guildhall Art Gallery, King Street, Cheapside
	Kenwood, The Iveagh Bequest, Hampstead Lane, NW3
	National Gallery, Trafalgar Square
	National Maritime Museum, Romney Road, Greenwich
	National Portrait Gallery, St Martin's Place, Trafalgar Square
	Percival David Foundation of Chinese Art, University of London
	The Tate Gallery, Millbank
	Victoria and Albert Museum, Cromwell Road
Manchester	City Art Gallery, Moseley Street
	Whitworth Art Gallery, Whitworth Park
Newcastle-upon-Tyne	Laing Art Gallery and Museum
Norwich	The Castle Museum
Nottingham	City Art Gallery and Museum (The Castle Museum)
Oxford	Ashmolean Museum, Beaumont Street
Salford	Museum and Art Gallery, Peel Park

Sheffield	Graves Art Gallery, Surrey Street
	Mappin Art Gallery, Weston Park
Southampton	Art Gallery, Civic Centre

There are very many other public art galleries in smaller towns, most of which have some pictures that are worth looking at. And nowadays you will be able to find commercial art galleries, not only in London and the larger cities, but also in small towns and even in villages. Although these little galleries do not have a permanent collection of their own, they show a variety of exhibitions of contemporary art, which are usually lively and enjoyable and well worth a visit. You can go in and look around without buying anything.

11 Books and journals that might be helpful and that you could enjoy looking at

Art for Children by Ana M. Berry, published by The Studio 1929, reprinted 1942

Art without Epoch by Ludwig Goldscheide, published by George Allen & Unwin 1937

Pictures in the Post by Richard Carline, published by Gordon Fraser 1959

Making a Poster by Austin Cooper, published by The Studio 1938, reprinted 1945

Pleasure from Pictures by Pamela Strain, published by The Studio 1950

The Story of Art by E. H. Gombrich, published by Phaidon Press

Shapes and Stories by Geoffrey Grigson, published by John Baker 1964

Shapes and Adventures by Geoffrey Grigson, published by John Baker 1967

Shapes and People by Geoffrey Grigson, published by John Baker 1969

Shapes and Creatures by Geoffrey Grigson, published by John Baker 1972

Understanding Art by Betty Churcher, published by Holmes McDougall 1973

Historic Houses, Castles and Gardens and *Museums and Art Galleries*, journals published by ABC Travel Guide every year

Acknowledgments

The author and publishers would like to thank the following for permission to reproduce illustrations:

The Trustees of the British Museum (Plates 1, 19, 25, 29, 41, 43, 47, 49, 53, 54, 55); The National Gallery (Plates 2, 4, 14, 15, 16, 17, 22, 33, 39, 40, 50, 51); Mr Edmond Kapp (Plates 28 and 30, by courtesy of David Wise, Esq., and the Dowager Lady Aberconway, Samuel Courtauld Collection, respectively); London Transport (Plates 5, 8, 9); British Rail (Plate 6); Department of the Environment (Plate 7, reproduced from the Highway Code by permission of the Controller, Her Majesty's Stationery Office); City of Manchester Art Galleries (Plates 38 and 52); Ferens Art Gallery, Kingston-upon-Hull (Plates 45 and 46); Leeds City Art Galleries (Plate 48); The Walker Art Gallery, Liverpool (Plates 23, 24, 27, 36); The Greater London Council as Trustees of the Iveagh Bequest, Kenwood (Plates 32 and 35); The General Post Office (Plate 10); Phaidon Press Ltd and the Victoria and Albert Museum (Plates 12 and 13); Victoria and Albert Museum (Plates 11 and 42); The Tate Gallery, London (Plates 3, 21, 26, 31, 34, 44, 57, 58); The Scottish National Gallery of Modern Art (Plates 59 and 60); Mr R. John (Plate 34); The Ashmolean Museum, Oxford (Plates 18 and 56); The Birmingham Museum and Art Gallery (Plates 20 and 37).

The local search series

Editor: Mrs Molly Harrison MBE,FRSA

This book is one of a highly successful series designed to help young people to look inquiringly and critically at particular aspects of the world about them. It encourages them to think for themselves, to seek first-hand information from other people, to make the most of visits to interesting places, and to record their discoveries and their experiences.

Many boys and girls enjoy detective work of this kind and find it fun to look for evidence and to illustrate their findings in ways that appeal to them. Such lively activities are equally rewarding whether carried out individually or in a group.

Already published

The English Village
Dennis R. Mills

Under the editorship of
Molly Harrison

The English Home
Molly Harrison

The Public Library
Frank Atkinson

Living Creatures of an English Home
Olive Royston

The Public Park
Herbert L. Edin

Farms and Farming
Rowland W. Purton

The Post Office
Olive Royston

Looking at the Countryside
Annesley Voysey

A Home of Your Own
Margaret Kirby

The Theatre
Olive Ordish

Graves and Graveyards
Kenneth Lindley

Rivers and Canals
Rowland W. Purton

Museums and Galleries
Molly Harrison

Markets and Fairs
Rowland W. Purton

Trees and Timbers
Herbert L. Edlin

Dress and Fashion
Olive Ordish

Looking at Language
J. A. Robinson

Factories, Forges and Foundries
Roy Christian

The Town Hall
Olive Royston

Seaside and Seacoast
Kenneth Lindley